Don't Squat With Yer Spurs On!

Don't Squat With Yer Spurs On!

A Cowboy's Guide To Life

Texas Bix Bender

GIBBS·SMITH
P
PUBLISHER

PEREGRINE SMITH BOOKS
SALT LAKE CITY

First printing September 1992
95 94 93   13 14 15 16 17 18 19 20

The quotations in this book come from a mixture of lore
and experience.

This is a Peregrine Smith Book, published by
Gibbs Smith, Publisher
P.O. Box 667
Layton, UT 84041

Manufactured in the U.S.A.
Design by Mary Ellen Thompson
Animation by Scott Greer, © 1992 by Gibbs Smith,
Publisher
Cover illustration by Fred Lambert
Interior illustrations: Katherine Field, pages 60, 128; Will
James (from *Cowboys North and South*, Charles Scribner's
Sons, © 1924), pages 4, 16, 20, 32, 34, 36, 38, 44, 46, 50,
58, 64, 68, 80, 82, 84, 86, 90, 92, 100, 102, 106, 114, 118,
126, 130, 132, 136, 138; Clint McRae, page 48; Frederic
Remington (from *Century Magazine* and *Ranch Life in the
Far West*), pages 12, 18, 42, 52, 70, 74, 98, 110, 112; L. E.
Wallis, pages 66, 88; all others clip art or unknown.

Library of Congress Cataloging-in-Publication Data
Bender, Texas Bix, 1949-
Don't squat with yer spurs on!: a cowboy's guide to life/
Texas Bix Bender.
p. cm.
ISBN 0-87905-470-0 (pb)
1. Cowboys—West (U.S.)—Humor. 2. West (U.S.)—Social
life and customs—Humor. 3. Cowboys' writings, Ameri-
can—West (U.S.)
I. Title.
F596.A75 1992
978—dc20   91-15213

CIP

THE CODE OF THE WEST

Write it in your heart. Stand by the code, and it will stand by you. Ask no more and give no less than honesty, courage, loyalty, generosity, and fairness.

Don't never interfere
with something that
ain't botherin' you none.

Timing has a lot to
do with the
outcome of a rain
dance.

Every quarrel is a private one. Outsiders are never welcome.

There never was a
horse that couldn't be
rode; there never was
a man that couldn't
be throwed.

There's more ways to
skin a cat than
stickin' his head in a
boot jack and jerkin'
on his tail.

Never ask a man the
size of his spread.

After weeks of beans and taters, even a change to taters and beans is good.

Some ranchers raise pigs and some will even admit it. Either way, they're raisin' pigs.

Never take to sawin' on the branch that's supportin' you, unless you're bein' hung from it.

Never kick a
fresh turd
on a hot day.

After eating an entire
bull, a mountain lion
felt so good he started
roaring. He kept it up
until a hunter came
along and shot him.
The moral: when you're
full of bull, keep your
mouth shut.

The easiest way to
eat crow is while
it's still warm.
The colder it gets,
the harder it is
to swaller.

If you find yourself
in a hole,
the first thing to do
is stop diggin'.

Never smack a man
who's chewin' tobacco.

If it don't seem like
it's worth the effort,
it probably ain't.

Never grumble. It makes you about as welcome as a sidewinder in a cow camp.

It don't take a genius
to spot a goat in
a flock of sheep.

When dealin' with a
slick son of a bitch,
start off by pinnin'
him down and changin'
his oil.

The biggest liar you'll
ever have to deal
with probably watches
you shave his face
in the mirror
every morning.

The best way to find
a lost stray is to go
to the place you would
go if you were a
lost stray.

Never ask a barber if
he thinks you need
a haircut.

If your guts have turned to fiddle strings on the cowboy trail, it ain't good for you and it ain't safe for me.

Never follow good
whiskey with water,
unless you're out of
good whiskey.

If you get to thinkin'
you're a person
of some influence,
try orderin' somebody
else's dog around.

Never try to run a
bluff when your
poke's empty.

Talk low,
talk slow,
and don't say too much.

A man with an
edgy smile is like a
dog with a waggin' tail:
he's not happy,
he's nervous.

Don't worry about biting off more than you can chew. Your mouth is probably a whole lot bigger 'n you think.

Good judgment comes
from experience,
and a lot of that comes
from bad judgment.

Always drink upstream from the herd.

Generally,
you ain't learnin' nothin'
when your mouth
is a-jawin'.

Tellin' a man to go to hell and makin' him do it are two entirely different propositions.

Makin' it in life is kinda
like bustin' broncs:
you're gonna get
thrown a lot.
The simple secret
is to keep gettin'
back on.

Never miss a chance to rest your horse.

The best way to cook
any part of a rangy
ol' longhorn is to toss
it in a pot with a
horseshoe, and when
the horseshoe is
soft and tender, you
can eat the beef.

Remain independent
of any source of
income that will
deprive you of your
personal liberties.

Generally speaking,
fancy titles and
nightshirts are a
waste of time.

Never drop your gun
to hug a grizzly.

Trust everybody in the
game, but always cut
the cards.

A woman's heart is
like a campfire.
If you don't
tend to it regular,
you'll soon lose it.

If you're ridin' ahead
of the herd, take a
look back every now
and then to make
sure it's still there.

When you give a lesson
in meanness to a critter
or a person, don't be
surprised if they learn
their lesson.

No matter where
you ride to,
that's where you are.

If you're gonna go,
go like hell.
If your mind's
not made up,
don't use your spurs.

If you're sittin' at a
counter eatin',
leave your hat on.
If you're sittin'
at a table,
take it off.

A body can pretend
to care,
but they can't
pretend to be there.

The best way to have quiche for dinner is to make it up and put it in the oven to bake at about 325 degrees. Meanwhile, get out a large T-bone, grill it, and when it's done, eat it. As for the quiche, continue to let it bake, but otherwise ignore it.

Some things
ain't funny.

A lot of good luck
is undeserved,
but then so is
a lot of bad luck.

It don't matter so much
how long a ride
you have, as how
well you ride it.

You can just about
always stand more 'n
you think you can.

When it comes to cussin'
don't swallow your tongue;
Use both barrels
And air out your lungs.

A man who
wants to loan you
a slicker
when it ain't rainin'
ain't doin' much
for you.

There's only two things
you need to be
afraid of:
a decent woman and
bein' left afoot.

Remember,
even a kick in the
caboose is a
step forward.

There's two theories
to arguin' with
a woman.
Neither one works.

If you're gonna drive
cattle through town, do
it on a Sunday. There's
little traffic and people
are more prayerful and
less disposed to
cuss at you.

If you expect to
follow the trail,
you must do your
sleepin' in the
winter.

Always try to be a bit nicer than is called for, but don't take too much guff.

There's no time to rest when there's work to be done. Eat on the run, forget about sleep, and change horses often.

Katherine Field -83

If you're gonna
take the measure
of a man,
take the full measure.

Don't take off too many clothes when you bed down on the trail. You might need to dress in a hurry.

Egg shells
in the coffee
keep it shy of
bitterness.

Always remember
your horse hears
and smells
a whole lot
more 'n you do.

Never
go to your room
in the daytime.

When you're tryin'
somethin' new,
the fewer people
who know about it,
the better.

Just because a man
takes his boots off
to go wadin'
don't mean he plans
to swim the Atlantic.

Kickin' never gets you
nowheres,
less'n you're a mule.

There's no place
'round the campfire
for a
quitter's blanket.

Only a buzzard
feeds on his friends.

Control your generosity
when you're dealin' with
a chronic borrower.

Don't squat
with yer
spurs on!

When you throw your
weight around,
be ready to have it
thrown around by
somebody else.

Speak your mind,
but ride a fast horse.

Too much debt
doubles the weight
on your horse
and puts another
in control of the reins.

There's no such thing
as a sure thing.
Let the other fellows
run on the rope
if they want to,
but you keep your
money in your pocket.

On the range,
an unlocked ranch
house is an invitation
to a weary cowboy
to help himself
to food and shelter.
Cash payment for this
kind of hospitality is a
serious breach of
etiquette. A note of
thanks and payment in
kind is all that
is expected.

No matter where you
go or what you do,
keep your saddle and
chaps and always know
where you can get a
good ride.

When you're puttin'
together an outfit, take
your time. Wait for all
the loose-lipped,
manicured cowboys
to run their line and
wander off. Then make
your picks from the
wiser heads who
stayed around listenin'
and thinkin'.

Go after life as if it's something that's got to be roped in a hurry before it gets away.

Workin' behind a plow,
all you see
is a mule's hind end.
Workin' from the
back of a horse,
you can see across the
country as far as your
eye is good.

Solvin' problems
is like throwin' cattle.
Dig your heels in
on the big ones
and catch the little ones
'round the neck.

Never ride with a
saddle stiff.
He will prey
on your honesty
and loyalty.

The only way
to drive cattle fast
is slowly.

The basics of roping
are a sense of rhythm,
good timing, and
an eye for distance.
You might also wanta
keep this in mind
when you're
two-steppin' around
the dance floor.

Never run from a fight.
If you're gonna get hit,
it's better to take it in the
front than in the back—
and it looks better.

Lettin' the cat
outta the bag
is a whole lot easier
'n puttin' it back.

Don't let so much reality
into your life
that there's no room
left for dreamin'.

Always take a good
look at what you're
about to eat.
It's not so important
to know what it is,
but it's critical
to know what it was.

Always carry more 'n
one rope.
You might run across
more 'n one rope
can handle.

A person who agrees
with all your palaver
is either a fool
or he's gettin' ready
to skin ya.

Ain't never seen
a wild critter
feelin' sorry for itself.

The quickest way
to double your money
is to fold it over
and put it
back in your pocket.

If you want to have a drink or two, that's all right—but don't wear out your boot soles on a brass rail.

The best way to
keep your word
is not to
give it foolishly.

Never miss a good chance to shut up.

If you drink tequila,
don't dive off the
sidewalk.
Most generally
the water is too low,
and in nine out of
ten towns,
there is at least a
$50 fine for it.

There's a lot more to
ridin' a horse
than just sittin' in the
saddle and lettin' yer
feet hang down.

Most folks are like a
bob-wire fence.
They have
their good points.

Nobody ever drowned himself in his own sweat.

No tree is too big
for a short dog
to lift his leg on.

You don't need decorated words to make your meanin' clear. Say it plain and save some breath for breathin'.

Two dry logs
will burn a green one.

If you work for a man,
ride for his brand.
Treat his cattle
as if they were
your own.

Never lie
unless you have to,
and if you don't have
a damn good lie,
stick to the truth.

When you get to where
you're goin',
the first thing to do
is take care of the
horse you rode in on.

To get a handle on modern French philosophers, just assume that everything nonphysical is real, while everything of substance is unreal. So, sadness is real, but escargot is not.

Honesty is not somethin'
you should flirt with—
you should be
married to it.

Wet dogs
are never welcome.

It doesn't matter how
fast you are if the other
guy is so much as
a hair faster.

Depending on the
circumstances,
you can tolerate a
certain amount of
slick-eared calf poachin',
but horse stealin' is
a hangin' offense.

You can't always tell a
gunslinger by the
way he walks.

Wear a hat with a brim
wide enough to shed
sun and rain, fan a
campfire, dip water,
and whip a fightin' cow
in the face.

Any cowboy worth his salt has a rope hand that itches clean up to his shoulder bone.

When you're pickin' a
workin' horse,
look for one named
Screwtail,
Stump Sucker,
Rat's Ass, Pearly Gates,
Liver Pill, or
Darlin' Jill. Leave the
Champions and Silvers
for the show ring.

You can never step in
the same river twice.

Never take another man's bet. He wouldn't offer it if he didn't know somethin' you don't.

Any time a large herd
moves through a
civilized area there's a
lot of shit to clean up.

Coolness and a steady nerve will always beat simple quickness. Take yer time and you'll only need to pull the trigger once.

A center-fire rig won't do
on steep trails. So when
you're in rimfire country,
always double-cinch
your saddle.

Never get up
before breakfast.
If you have to get up
before breakfast,
eat breakfast first.

If you want to forget all your troubles, take a little walk in a brand-new pair of high-heeled ridin' boots.

Comin' as close to the truth as a man can come without actually gettin' there is comin' pretty close, but it still ain't the truth.

Never joke with mules
or cooks as they have
no sense of humor.

The first thing to do
when you get up in the
morning is put on
your Stetson.

Don't get mad at somebody who knows more 'n you do. It ain't their fault.

It's best to keep
your troubles pretty
much to yourself,
'cause half the people
you'd tell 'em to won't
give a damn,
and the other half will
be glad to hear
you've got 'em.

Don't ask friends for
more 'n they would give
on their own.

It's better to sit on your horse and do nothing than to wear him out chasin' shadows.

Pick the right horse
for the job.

The cowboy who
exaggerates too much
soon finds that
everyone else has left
the campfire.

It's rare to find a horse
that everyone agrees is
the best in the herd.

A subtle joke about a man's character can ruin a reputation faster than an obvious lie.

Nothin's better than a cool drink of water—but too much can give you a bellyache.

The length of a
conversation don't tell
nothin' about the
size of the intellect.

A smart ass
just don't
fit in a saddle.

No matter who
says what,
don't believe it
if it don't make sense.

The wildest critters
live in the city!